Lanterns Of Thoughts

A collection of heartwarming poems

Prabuddha Ray

BookLeaf
Publishing

India | USA | UK

Made with ❤ on the BookLeaf Publishing Platform
www.bookleafpub.in
www.bookleafpub.com

Dedication

To every soul traversing this winding path of life-

may you find the light to guide you through darkness
the courage to smile, even in pain
the power to push through the hardships ahead

I hope you find shelter and comfort in these poems,
for these are dedicated to you, who dares to enjoy life
to the fullest.

Preface

*Life is not a straight road — it's a winding path of light
and shadow, joy and ache, beginnings and farewells.*

*This collection of poems is a reflection of that journey —
the pauses between breaths, the unspoken words, the
small wonders we often overlook.*

*Each poem was written in a moment of truth — some
fleeting, some eternal. Together, they form a map of the
heart: fragile, flawed, but deeply alive.*

Acknowledgements

This book would not have come to life without the beautiful people who stayed beside me through my ups and downs and made me who I am today.

To my family who has been motivating me throughout my journey, to my friends who make me laugh and have stayed beside me, and to all the readers who find a piece of themselves in these poetries- I am really grateful to you all.

Your love and presence gave me the ink and life to these poems.

Lastly, I want to thank Thammi, Dadu and Baba for always supporting me, teaching me the core values of life and giving me strength and love to travel on this beautiful journey of life. Your lessons still continue to live through me, in lessons I am still discovering. I miss you all.

1. The Journey

Countless sailors of Dreamland voyaged across the sea of
tranquility
The night sang the sonata
And scripts of the life's escapades,
The moon and the stars glistened across the unlit sky,
Unraveling the path of the expedition ahead;
The painter rested on the shore in serenity,
Closing his eyes,
Embracing the conception he created.

2. Thoughts of an Overthinker

My mind is drifting across the restless sea
Diving in the waves of eternal chaos
Where the horizon seems like a pleasant vista
Yet my soul collides with an invisible mirror
Blocking the path towards serenity.

Where the heart loses in a battle of tug-and-war
Solutions stray around like dust particles left behind
Memories dazzle like a night club,
Dim and trippy, floating around like orbs.

'What ifs' and 'Do they' play like cassettes,
Replaying and revisiting scenes from the time gone
Trailer of coming days hover in the mind's corner
Possibilities and expectations flash like colours
Of a distant painting on a blank canvas.

But there's a corner that lights up my soul
A power, or a blessing, or a vision it is

That dwells inside, like a sixth sense;
Where I see the pain behind your smile,
The struggle behind your success,
The words behind your silence,
The truth that you keep hidden,
In the corner of your soul.

The heart feels heavy, the mind is at a race,
But I hold onto this feeling,
Feeling to move ahead with my powers and thoughts.
I see the horizon ahead, it is alluring;

I sense the calmness, the warmth,
The beauty in the little things.
I smile, with eyes glowing like a firefly
Breathing and moving ahead,
A destiny worth conquering.

3. Dance of the Fireflies

I saw the dance of the fireflies
In a realm where stars shimmer low,
Where the moon beacons the blue stream,
The cool breeze feels like a mystic dream.

I wandered through the vibrant mist,
Startled by swerving dim lights far,
When I came across the fireflies' play
Dancing with a shimmering grace.

Their lights twirled, like blinking stars
Their wings fluttered, and hummed with the flowing
stream;
Like little fairies visiting the beautiful abode,
As little fireworks healing the soul, and painting hope.

They twirled and leaped, with the hymn of the night
Like an orchestra in play, a poetry in motion,
Like an art alive, mesmerizing to the eyes,
Felt like a warm embrace, tugging the strings of heart.

A charming night, under the beaming moon,
Witnessed a symphony of pure delight,
Time stood still, the soul could feel,
The enchanting dance of the fireflies.

4. A Light for the Soul

If I bring you the shades from a painting
Would it make you smile like a child?
If I bring you the colours from a flower
Would you feel happier?
If I could shine your path with the light from the stars
Would you be able to traverse
Through the darkness, through the pain
Prettier and merrier?

If I could make you perceive
The aroma of the shining dawn,
The shimmer of the morning dew,
The play of the butterflies,
The dance of the daisies,
The symphony of the dreamy wind,
Would it make you feel at ease?
To close your eyes,
And settle within the gratifying décor
And let the nature encircle you
To let you feel serenity.

If I could let you witness,
The hymn of the wrecking waves
The vibrance of the setting sun,
The shifting of shimmering sand,
Would you sit beside me,
And be a part of this placid theatre?
Leave behind the jumble,
The traction, the constraint
And feel poised for a moment
To cherish the other world,
And smile to your heart's content.

5. A Dusk's Tale

The sun has draped the vermillion attire
Beaming behind the mountains, like a scorching fire.
As it gently retires like a magician's last dance
Painting the skies in an orange trance.
The birds returning to their nests in threes and fours
The blue stream glides, humming across the shores.
The autumn dew drops frolic on nature's bed,
The hues of the greens fade into murky silhouettes.
The farmers saunter, with the cattle towards their doors
And tell their little ones the fairies' lores;
Far away on a branch the last robin sang,
The snack vendor is selling his last batch with a clang.

6. A Walk in Rain

It was a blissful evening;
The rain was in a mood to sing,
The raging clouds proclaimed to be present;
The flickering dust tones leisurely turned evanescent.
The yellow poppies by the roadside,
Swayed, as if relishing the vibe.
The cuckoo sang far in some nook
The raindrops painted the nature's look
They walked in the vibe, adrift in glory,
The twilight witnessed a graceful story.

7. An Urban Ordeal

"Slow down, slow down"
Hollered someone from afar,
Restrained my pace, looked crosstown
Drenched in sweat, huffing in the char,
Saw an old man in tattered shirt
Limping in his soiled pants,
As his beaming eyes fixated on my cast;
He had an eccentric feature, even in his old
His moiety features hid in the cold.

I approached the man, in frantic
With my mind drowning in a state of erratic
"Why are you rushing?", asked the man
I replied, "Need to hurry somewhere, if I can."
"Will you spare some minute?", he sought.
Bewildered me replied, "I can, what's your thought?"

"What do you see, when time slows down?"
I smirked and said, "I don't know, it must be lown."
"Breathe slow, and let it flow,

What do you see, in this afterglow?"
"Vessels, and masses goading," I said
"What else can you see in this spread?"
"Commotion and pollution widespread."

His eyes glowed, as the old man said,
"Do you see?
The little girl selling flowers in this spread?"
"The suited man alike you walking with a bouquet?"
"The white dog with the lad, wanting to play?"
"The orange cat wagging its tail, asking for a bite?"
"The kids running on the pavement, holding kites?"
"The old uncle sitting on the bench, going through
news?"
"The tea-seller counting heads, while the tea brews?"
"The mother consoling her child, who tumbled upon the
rock?"
"The old souls holding hands and going out for a walk?"

Overwhelmed, and dazed,
I answered the man as he gazed,
"I see everyone around, what's your intent?"
He smiled, and replied with a heavy accent,
"I see you rushing to and fro, day in and out,
Breathless, restless, a man so stout;
Why not slow down, breath slow, and look around?
The joy in little things around you can be found."

"Wake up early, begin your morning with a smile,
Little changes will enrich your lifestyle,
Freshen up, walk right, bask in the morning sun,
And uncover the colours of life, the essence of real fun.
You seemed wise, someone really nice
Lest you wouldn't be bearing with me,
My words wouldn't have been sufficed."

Time seemed to have consumed me,
And teleported me in a portal, only I could see,
Swimming in deadlines, pressure and pain,
I had lost the way towards my destination.
My mind was playing tapes of my trudges,
Breathless, monotonous, drowning in the sea of drudges.

Found a pedestal, rested still, raised my hands towards
the sky,
Respired slow, tried grasping the dot of light floating
high;
The world around me seemed cracking,
As rays of light shattered through the dark walls,
Collapsing the veil, a hearty breeze twirling.
The noise, the clatter had restored,
The lights flashed, the rides roared.
I gazed around, seeking for the old man,
He had faded, somewhere in the urban clan.

Hands shaking, seeping, numb, as I stood in the pathway,
A kid tugged my pants, lending a water bottle, and
asked,
"Are you okay?"
Dumbfounded, and spooked,
I asked the kid, "Did you see the old man, present with
me, chatting?"
The kid, baffled, replied shockingly,
"You were standing alone, and babbling!"

8. Be Free

Close your laptop, keep away your phone
Open the window, and see the moon;
Stars are gleaming, seeing your face
As you dissolve with outdoors, far from the race.
Put on your joggers, have a quick stroll
Feel the breeze, let the nature unroll
Sit on the grass, gaze at the flowers' dance
Lie down, close your eyes, and immerse in nature's
trance.
Sit by the window, watch the droplets roll,
Relish your favourite drink, and replenish your soul.
Pack your bags, and travel the extra mile
Mountains, valleys, and beaches will make you smile.

9. The Bridge Between Us

Between your heart and mine,
Lies a bridge, serene and divine,
Bound by strings of eternal fate,
Where our spirits meet, our hearts elate.

Your eyes find mine; time stops as we gaze,
Our hands intertwine, the distance fades.
Through thick and thin, through night and day,
Our hearts beat as one, all along the way.

No wind can shake the bridge between us,
Two souls together, no storm can crush,
Even if you stay away somewhere far
I'll find your heart- wherever you are.

10. School Days

(For my dear friends)

I walk past the gates of my school
In tucked shirt, messy spikes
Wondering about the day's routine

Morning light enters through the window
Half dusted board exhibit last day's tasks
Some familiar calls catch my attention,
As I put down my bags
And huddle with my buddies for a quick gossip,
And we hear the bell again;

Teacher arrives, calls everyone's name
Lining up to attend the morning assembly
Prayers, pledge, and speeches goes
As we stood as a part in line
Waiting for the bell for class;

Classes progressed, one by one

Subjects changed, teachers changed
Books filled with pencil scribblings
Notebooks filled with writings and red ticks,
With last pages becoming the students' corner

Waited for the recess gong,
For which we used to crave for long,
And then opened the tiffin boxes,
And also anecdotes, more gossips,
As hands flung from one tiffin to another
With chuckles and filling tummies,
Corridors and premises crammed with shuffles
Chatters and laughter echoed the corners.

Do you remember?
The wait for the games period?
Dividing teams, putting on shoes,
Jerseys gradually occupied the desk
Legs tapping, excitement blooming
And with the bell, we rushed to change
We rushed to ground
To run around with the ball and play
Playing like there's no tomorrow
Galloping, sweating, and celebrating.

The Annual Ceremony had its own chapter of fun
From bunking classes, to evading teachers

From being involved in decorations, to participations
Playing with colours and papers
Dressing up and vibing alongwith songs and dance
As days filled with ecstasy passed by in a fling.

Doodles in notebooks and benches,
Imperfect equations, imperfect dreams
Sharing benches, sharing tiffin
Life was so wholesome back then.

Teachers formed a special bond with us,
From fear of getting scolded, to getting pats for good
grades
Exam tension, standing in corridors
Anxiety on result days
At the end of the day, they always stayed beside us
Supporting, motivating as we progressed.

Laughing together, crying together
Innocent life, filled with hopes and needs
From secret keepings to secret crushes
Blooming love and heartbreaks
The classroom and corridors remember them all.

Last benches were something special, weren't they?
From intellectual gossips, to planning pranks
To avoid teachers, to forming a band,

Singing songs, beating benches
The walls were painted with our stories.

Farewell became bittersweet
The last day in school,
The last day of a chapter in our lives,
Smiles spread, hugs and handshakes went along
But the heart felt heavy, words became supressed
As we smiled at each other,
Wishing we would stay in touch always
The last photo was clicked,
The last bell rang.

As I walked through the corridors again,
I saw the child me running with his notebook,
As I entered the classroom,
The walls seemed to remember me,
Sitting on the bench, I perceived the recollections play
around me,

The world around me was small,
But felt like a safe place,
The walls and the bench had preserved the scribblings
The green board partially had names written in white
chalks
It was that sunlit room,
Where we used to be innocent and loud

Then I hear teacher call my name,
The last bell rang,
I woke up.

11. A Day In The Mountains

The sound of the Thrush broke my slumber
With eyes heavy as the cold;
The rays are peeping through the window curtains
It was chilly, yet cozy.

As I dragged myself out, on the porch
The serene vista welcomed me
The hills were vivid,
Clouds were swaying with the breeze
The barbets were singing in some distant branches
The thrushes were playing on the front roof
The Sun was playing hide-and-seek among the clouds
The pines and cedars hummed and creaked;

The tea complimented the cold
As I looked around,
The mountain lady was in the local gardens
Plucking fresh morning harvests
The old gentleman was feeding the goats
As they jumped on him, excited with the hay

The hens twirled around, pecking
As little drizzles coloured the canvas around;

Walking on the stony and muddy path,
The petrichor hit me;
Buttercups and daisies swerved in the drizzles
As it painted lush around
The fog draped like an old blanket
Some children were standing on the sideways
Hairs combed, bags on their backs
Giggling and wondering far
Waiting for their school van.

The town felt like out of a film scene,
Blushing in the blues,
Some feet away, flowing water orchestrated the
backdrop
Footsteps and voices echoed around the drenched road,
As souls unveiled from within the dense haze
The aroma of hot momos and chai dawdled in the breeze,
As I became a captive there for some hours.

The ascending path bent into the wilderness
The fog decked out the hinterland
Shuffles and huffs accompanied my shadow
Tails wagging, dense furs swaying,
As they sniffed around,

And guided me for some miles,
Water droplets slipped gracefully from the umbrella
As I trekked towards my abode;

As the skies turned golden,
Hills draped a blue duvet in the far horizon;
The Sun's last glance illuminated the tranquility
The rays flashed like brushstrokes,
Painting the nature in amber hues
Pines whispered silence around me,
The old man was cutting branches for fire,
As the lady assembled and took them inside the hut;
The thrush performed its last song
Before bidding adieu for the day.

The last sip of tea felt entrancing
As the hills scintillated dim lights far
The stars made me feel small and comforting,
Like millions of fireflies frozen in time;
The cold caught up to my shadow in the porch light
The cicadas and moths performed in the flamboyant
twilight
Obscure echoes hummed behind the boundaries,
I concluded my paperback,
Closed my eyes and drifted into oblivion.

12. Inside The Mind

It's dark, as I creep along the narrow alley
I hear whispers and ruffles,
As I head towards the silent valley
The lights on the corner flickered in pain,
The moths danced for survival,
In the pouring rain.

Bricks have aged, greens have invaded
The finger stains on glasses,
With sweeping time, have abraded
The frigid embraced my soul,
The silence engulfed the town,
While the ghoul set out on a stroll.

Thorns on the alley broached skin deep,
Shattered voices and wails loomed from the keep
A devious siren dappled the sky red,
Shadows jived and feasted on dread.
The maze imbued with an obscure hymn
The poet in the corner scribbled in grim.

A beam of light traversed from far,
Like a blessing from an angel, a medicine for the scars
A ballad of the fairies in a drought struck ground
Frightened the shadows of the fear eating hounds.
A hand touched the wounds of the frigid spirit,
A warm embrace for the bruised heart to inherit.

13. Time

Life is so pleasant
You wake up, with the dance of the sunrays
Glare outdoors, with your mug of coffee
As you see the man in suit with a briefcase,
Sprinting, to catch the bus by the junction
The swallows are soaring high,
Bathing in the morning sonata
You smile,
Time ticks away.

Lazing in the sofa, with munchies
You invade the digital world;
Colours flashed across the yellow walls
The sun departed with nightfall,
Silence diffused;
As you cherish your youth,
Time was ticking away.

You're grooving in the rain,
You're devoured by the medleys,

When you see the man in suit, drenched
Scampering towards his residence;
Lightning struck,
As you tumbled, lying on the floor
You're spooked by your reflection on the glass
Sitting in melancholy,
Time was ticking away.

The dawning was somber,
You have missed the sun,
You have wrinkles, bruises on your ankles
You have turned cadaverous;
You see the man smiling,
Celebrating with his family
The swallows flew low,
As they glared at you and left;
Time was ticking away.

You dashed for the bus,
In cluttered clothes and messy hair,
But the bus had departed,
With no traces of a next one
Flowers and leaves had parched,
The world around you was turning blue
The dusk was about to consume you
As you fell to your knees,
In tears, in agony

Time has ticked away.

14. A Better World

What if this world was a paradise?
No pain, no sacrifice
Peace would be the power,
Decorated with beautiful trees and flowers,
Life would be happier, without any glower.

Climate would be pure
Pollution won't exist anymore,
Habitat would bloom in symphony
Birds and animals will live in harmony
Streams will be blue,
As seen in picture books
The world would adorn a beautiful look.

There won't be any poverty,
People won't die hungry,
Education would be focal,
Rights for folks would be equal;
Crimes would cease to prosper
With no conflicts, no war

Employments would be feast,
Migrations would be ceased
Envision a world without corruption
A better world without disruption.

15. Paper Planes

An afternoon painted in amber hues
The sun setting behind the urban monolith,
Rush in the far, in a junk-soaked city
Stayed two souls,
In intimate towers, but hearts far
Strangers to the city
Strangers to each other.

Walking across the marbled rooftop
Relishing the twilight tints,
When the ambiance collided with a peculiar presence
Baffled by her demeanour in the closing tower
As she gracefully accreted dried garments,

Appalled by her innocence and allure,
Whose smile shined the prettiest that twilight,
As if the moon had decided to blossom early,
Time ceased for a moment,
The silence felt like the loudest beat,
When she caught his stolid stare

Her glory dissolved into angst
When the dusk witnessed a glaring war;
Time rushed in streams,
Leaves and twigs swirled with the gale,
As they receded to their camps,
Memories entwined in their play.

He was confounded,
She was too,
He wanted to know her more,
She wasn't sure;
Both were wallflowers in an animated setting,
Seeking for novel escapades;
The script had been penned
The twilight had veiled a poignant tale.

A new sundown drew a lone shadow,
Her presence was truant,
Deeming perturbed and disjoined,
He was drowning in contrition
When the last sunrays flashed,
The thrush proclaimed the dusk,
With its song of optimism;
The breeze was a sage's blessing,
The dove duplets assured his soul.

Rushing down the stairs to his abode,

Vibrant sheets on the table caught his glance,
He opted to craft a paper plane,
Entailing an approach to her;
The plane soared the cobalt skies,
As it landed in her abode,
He loitered for her response.
When the moon draped the daylight's end.

The ensuing twilight touched down with a plane,
With a message of assent for his staunch heart,
He was rejoiced,
She was too,
She treasured his intent,
He was engulfed in her smile,
Embracing her akin response.

The glaring war resumed again,
The parleys coloured the evening,
Eyes glowed like pearls in deep blue sea,
Smiles gleamed like silver lining in the autumn skies
The thrush and doves cheered their conclave,
The twilight dawned a heartfelt anecdote,
As the two planes stayed still,
Facing each other.

16. The Song of the Sailor

The gulls mourn the dawn of the tranquil sea,
The sun melts gold, setting me free,
The hull reeks doused lumber and old brine,
The hard breeze hums for the soul of mine.

O deep seas, how weary yet mighty you seem,
Your spirit haunts every dastard's dream,
You embrace me in lows, you hurl me in highs,
You dare me to face you, reciting your war cry.

Sails set high, like white ghosts in daylight,
The frigid cold breathing is testing my might,
My soul is burning with the wounds and scars,
But I am a dreamer, soaring very far.

I have barged my way, through hot Atlantic tempest,
My keel is enduring the sea's tempers in this wild quest.
I have battled with the spirits of titan gales,
I have witnessed the twilight dance of the whales.

Some nights have come to me to slay,
The sea has claimed my mate as her prey;
He won't return, sea won't repay,
I burn the cigar, to heal my scars away.

The wound has cut deep, as I hummed in pain,
I clutched my spirits and sailed towards the terrain;
The calmness grasped the sea, the stars glinted bright,
The waves orchestrated the hymn of the night.

The moon is guiding me through the murky haze,
I am fighting with my scars and pride as my heart
decays.
The sea calls for my soul through her plea,
The grand waves crashed on the deck, she wants me.

17. The Train to Utopia

The rusty station borders the abysmal shore,
Waves narrating tales from the ancient lore,
Gulls shrieking as the sun dazzles far,
A traveller rests on the bench, waiting for his railcar.

The silent platform echoes the breaths of wild
The squirrel plays and peeks over like a child
Dolphins twirl in the gleaming yellows
The autumn felt placid and mellow.

The sun is dimming, tardily by the horizon
Painting hues of orange to the dreamy season.
In the distance, a faint call of train is heard,
With the clouding lights, the sound gets blurred.

A journey unknown, to the land of the stars
As the tinted pages gets scribbled in his memoir,
The breeze twirls, with raining sparkles of salt
The rails bend far into the twilight's gestalt.

A passage stands devoid, with no ride in vision
The heart beats and tidal waves synchronize in collision,
Whispers of the night patronize the soul
The lone traveller sets out on a stroll.

The clock has stopped, hands decaying with time
The window panes and benches are veiled with grime
The flora has proclaimed the tiles as its realm,
The outworn name has been a captive of time's helm.

Resting himself on a bench, he dives in his mind's sea
Counting stars, waiting to be free;
He smiles, as he basks in the fireflies' dazzle,
Wishing to see the lights, waiting for his journey's yell.

The sea hums with its song of eternity,
The beauty of waiting and the wild formed an affinity.
The traveller closes his eyes, reflections turning clear,
The train to Utopia honks, it is finally here.

18. Music, Our Soulmate

Music, a guardian, soft and strong,
It stays beside us, through right and wrong.
It lifts the spirits, when darkness creeps
And guides the soul, through restive sleep.

It heals the wounds, where words don't serve,
It unbinds the knots, when life goes swerve.
It calms the heart, when it falls to grief
It appeases the mind, like a balm of relief.

When life drowns in a sea of sorrows,
Music as a lighthouse shows us the path to tomorrow,
With every note, it brings colours to soul,
Like a true friend, music stays with us all.

19. Be Kind

Kindness is like a real power,
That heals a heart, in pain or sour.
Like a blessing that cures an ache,
A warm light when life turns opaque.

Like a gentle breeze of an autumn afternoon,
It soothes the soul, like a natural boon,
Like the serenity of a full Moon,
Feels pleasing to you, like a magical tune.

It is found in the joy of little things,
In the hearty smile of passing beings,
A soothing word in the veil of gloom,
A beautiful sunrise, a flower's bloom.

Give them a call, give them a warm embrace,
Listen to their thoughts, stay with their pace.
Smile at people, compliment them,
Tell your family, how much you love them.

Help them with their chores, make them smile,
Help an elderly person lessen their work pile,
Feed an animal, plant a tree,
Live a tip or donate, let your soul be free.

May you give, may you share,
Little spores of kindness everywhere,
A soft gesture in joy and strife,
Kindness is the art of life.

20. A Family Canvas

In the brink of night, where silence speaks,
Under a dim lit lamp, a painter seeks
A brush in hand, a restless grace,
A canvas reflecting his family's face.

A sea of hope hides the storm inside,
The canvas waits- white and wide;
Each line a memory, each stroke a prayer,
A frame reflecting love and care.

His wife's soft smile, her pretty eyes,
Like the warmth of a beautiful sunrise;
Embraces their little child's innocence,
As the night hums a heartfelt resonance.

Time flies, night collapses into light,
Shades play around, love takes flight,
His calloused hands, and tired frame,
Still bows to his soul's burning flame.

He learnt to perceive through strokes and ache
He pours his soul in his mural, for their sake.
As the hues mature, in lines and sweeps,
He could see their faces, a connection so deep.

Shirts splattered in paints, hands shivering,
Tears rolled down, his colours were breathing.
They were smiling, glaring at him,
Alive with love, in the twilight dim.

The serene evening answered a heart's call,
His family sits eternal, on the front wall,
A smile adorned his face, his hands had heard his plea,
Brushes laid down, his soul is set free.

21. Pathway to Peace

Let the souls meet by the horizon,
Where the sky and sea converge;
The waves murmur and swash,
The brisk breeze soothes the soul,
Shimmering stars embellish the ambience,
Sands sparkle like diamonds on a treasure island.

Let the souls meet by the horizon,
Where fireflies dance with the nature's ecstasy,
The nightingale's symphony engulfs the paradise,
The distance wails of whales conjures a sensation,
Where blue heavens paint the canvas of life,
Peace narrates a poignant poetry to the soul.

Because it is chaos out here
The yellow pages being still in mutiny,
The clamour cult consuming the cityscape,
Expansions tearing down the tranquility,
Rush confronting the race of time,
The loved ones contemplating the perished peace.